PRAISE FOR JASPREET SINGH

"This book stretches us towards deep time with immediate presence and tender precision. Such brilliant offerings and necessary reminders of our humanity, Singh's poems place us in companionship with the limber and the lithic, an interspecies assemblage from the minuscule to the massive. I'm grateful for how Singh brings together so many beloved poets and beings, so spaciously yet intimately, through *The Time of the Earth*."

—**RITA WONG**, award-winning author of *forage*

"These poems are profound and elemental: a 'water language' that dissolves, rushes, laps, meanders through time and varieties of silence into the unlit, unattainable, prelinguistic reaches of consciousness. A breathtaking collection."

—**JULIE SEDIVY**, award-winning author of *Linguaphile: A Life of Language Love*

"Jaspreet Singh's poems nourish our contemplation of the ephemeral and the eternal, the pebble and the mountain, water and its hidden language. Within this state of intense receptivity, mysteries of deep time unfurl alongside the import of everyday objects. The result of his poetic concentration is an uncanny realignment—"how close yet how invisible"—of the world around us."

—**DAVID MARTIN**, award-winning author of *Kink Bands*

"This book is an exquisite invitation to become absorbed in the flow and loops of experience. It offers us lines and imagery to return to, time and time again."

—**ALICE MAJOR**, award-winning poet of *Knife on Snow*

"Jaspreet Singh's precision with word and line reflects the rigour of this thought when he writes 'a voice/ repeats how inseparable we are from what we see/ as separate.' Singh threads imagery of the present time, geologic time, and water time, reiterating the brevity of human time throughout this new collection."

—**MARILYN DUMONT**, award-winning author of *that tongued belonging*

"A Keats for the Anthropocene, Jaspreet Singh reclaims Negative Capability as poetry's mandate. Sometimes 'I,' sometimes 'he' or even 'you,' Singh's speaker is polymorphous and polyphonic, a shapeshifting listener. His very line and stanza spacings expand our shrinking world by suggesting proximities and distances contrary to our colonial notions of what belongs to whom. The simplest domestic acts, the smallest bodies, contain the cosmos. 'Bees dream . . ./This is all we know/and all we can ever know.' This is the beautiful poetry we need now."

—**NATANIA ROSENFELD**, author of *Wild Domestic* and *The Blue Bed*

"*The Time of the Earth* brims with vivid experiments in versification, imagery, and typography. A virtuoso work, it shimmers as the crowning achievement of Singh's kaleidoscopic trilogy on the poetics of deep time."

—**RAJI SONI**, lecturer in English at the University of Toronto

"Jaspreet Singh's *The Time of the Earth* is a clear-eyed and eloquent examination of complicity and survivorship in the climate crisis. His poems hold political upheaval, social crisis, and environmental devastation in close and vital conversation; they attend to an unfolding awareness of the past and lay it alongside the bright shiv of the impending future in ways that spark both beauty and irreconcilable longing."

—**JENNA BUTLER**, award-winning author of *Revery: A Year of Bees*

THE

TIME

OF

THE

EARTH

BOOKS BY JASPREET SINGH

POETRY

The Time of the Earth (2026)
Dreams of the Epoch & the Rock (2024)
How to Hold a Pebble (2022)
November (2017)

MEMOIR

My Mother, My Translator (2021)

NOVELS

Face (2022)
Helium (2013)
Chef (2008)

SHORT STORIES

Seventeen Tomatoes: Tales from Kashmir (2004)

CHAPBOOK

Otolith (2026)

The Time of the Earth

POEMS

Jaspreet Singh

NeWest Press

Library and Archives Canada Cataloguing in Publication
Title: The time of the Earth : poems / Jaspreet Singh.
Names: Singh, Jaspreet, 1969– author.
Series: Crow said poetry ; 16.
Description: Series statement: Crow said poetry ; 16
Identifiers: Canadiana 20260159409 | ISBN 9781774391464 (softcover)
Subjects: LCGFT: Poetry.
Classification: LCC PS8637.I53 T56 2026 | DDC C811/.6—dc23

Editor for the Press: Laurie Graham
Book design: Natalie Olsen, Kisscut Design

NeWest Press wishes to acknowledge that the land on which we operate is Treaty 6 territory and a traditional meeting ground and home for many Indigenous Peoples, including Cree, Saulteaux, Niits-itapi (Blackfoot), Métis, and Nakota Sioux since time immemorial.

Canada Council for the Arts | Conseil des Arts du Canada
Funded by the Government of Canada | Financé par le gouvernement du Canada
Canada
access COPYRIGHT FOUNDATION
Alberta Government
Edmonton
edmonton arts council

NeWest Press acknowledges the support of the Canada Council for the Arts, the Government of Alberta through the Ministry of Arts, Culture and Status of Women and the Edmonton Arts Council for support of our publishing program. We acknowledge the financial support of the Government of Canada through the Canada Book Fund for our publishing activities.

NEWEST PRESS
10131 97 Street
Edmonton, Alberta T5J 0L2
780.432.9427
www.newestpress.com

Printed and bound in Canada.

For Helmut Weissert, earth scientist

And now I know that the time of human generations is not like the time of the earth

CZESŁAW MIŁOSZ

Human nature is an interspecies relationship

ANNA TSING

Why do we acknowledge only our textual sources but not the ground
we walk, the ever-changing skies, mountains and rivers, rocks and trees, the
houses we inhabit and the tools we use, not to mention the innumerable companions,
both non-human animals and fellow humans, with which and with whom we share our lives?

TIM INGOLD

CONTENTS

HOW UNATTAINABLE EARTH IS

How unattainable the deep earth is
how close yet how invisible

We still have no name for the pebble that liberates it-
self from a conglomerate No words for differences

between the smell of the sea
in summer and the smell of the sea in winter

I have been told one styrofoam cup
is not the anthropocene   but a billion
cups are

The most peaceful
moment today: When the waves
like little hands on a radio dial
    tuned   my breath   An otter
came out and started looking
at its dwelling place and there was nothing
that was not water

For a while I forgot the archipelago
of oligarchs   For a while
the horizon
line didn't seem uncanny

And now I am walking by some crumbling
window   Is that deep time
carboniferous in the fireplace?
Tonight I'm not in a judging mood

I simply swerve away as the little child's mother
tangling with fire
makes porridge and lullabies

WINTER DIALOGUES

In half-proper gear
the old man steps out toward the cafe   a short
morning walk on re-frozen snow-

slush   Half-dark sky   passing
cars lighting the way   His thoughts
still mushy with three-day-old news—
the 13,000 mile long journey of a humpback
whale   from the Pacific to some-
where near Zanzibar
in search of krill

He grew up not reading Homer
Some Mahabharata   Ramayana
did enter his ears as a child
But his myths were basically mountains
        and different
forms of water   Childhood—
so full of people
who walked or drove   without consulting
maps   One looked
at a paper map only when there was some border
trouble   or when the other
side   or his own   redrew the map

and at this new place where he has
lived now much longer than the old place
most people awakened
this morning

listening to the other side's wet
dream   *the border will be altered*

By a stop sign
on an empty park bench
hiding under a lost scarf
the oil company's logo

He waddles toward
the cafe no longer with the whale
almost forgets to congratulate
himself for not falling

Winter has arrived here
although *winter* and *here*
no longer mean the same

DARKNESS

what is water in the eyes of water

—Alice Oswald

All day water has waited for
Darkness to fall on it
In the dark

Oceans awaken in a different
Language
There's a whale

Under the waves
And a whale
Over the waves

The confusion of the day
The tree   the clouds
Were they within   water

Or reflected?
Only in the dark   other
Reflections become possible

Eyes collaborate with ears
The way they should
Deepening

Humility   Only in the dark
          Water listens
                    To time's hesitation   Not one but

All time   and feels
          Only the pulse   saying nothing
                    Then something

When the moment comes
          Everywhere and everywhen will
                    Crawl into water's ears

Like oxidized punctuation
  They'll pause and praise
    What needs to be praised

Darkness is not born
  Of absence of photons
    Or some other caged absence

Like a friend says darkness is
  Water's method Ripples waiting to be
    Touched by long dead stars

Perhaps it's the other
Way around—
Darkness rises

On water from water
Where is it housed   The history
Of water written by water?

Is a "layer"   a "border"   for water?
What is a "name"
For water?

The whale dives
Deeper and deeper
Past the abyssal and

Hadal zones
Nothing ever changes
And nothing

Remains the same And we come
Much later— So incomplete the echoes
Of our “ancient” conch shells

In the dark   water corrects
Mistranslations
Openness replaces *nothingness*

In the dark   a balance
Of stories   Curtains of fear open
Curtains of fear's absence

Darkness on water means water
Is lost in deep thought   On behalf
Of everyone water is thinking

EARTH WINDOW

A two-hundred-thousand-year-old woman
on a step ladder
recycling ochre

She pours me history in a wine glass
and for a moment it disappears   the gap
between the word for time and time

LICHEN

...at five in the afternoon in the
shadow of the only standing building in
the ghost town of Paldi I think about the
red tea lichen and bring to mind the script
lichen, the scribble lichen, the lung
lichen, the comma lichen, the candle
lichen, the orange wall lichen, the map
lichen, the flask lichen, the earth foam
lichen, the sunken disk lichen, the stubble
lichen, the thread lichen, the button
lichen, the navel lichen, the firedot
lichen, the fragile coral lichen, the
powdered sunshine lichen, the vagrant
lichen. [The ethnobotanist's phrases still
hover
around me especially here where
migrants from a far continent had built a
small temple.] When I was growing up
the boundary between sapiens and
lichens was hard and now it is not. But I
have never believed a
lichen blindfolds a rock. I believe
lichens are the eyes
the ears the flaming tongues of every
rock — the boundary-witness. Thought-
buildings start crouching within me.
Ancient songs run through histories of
symbiosis and some grand collaborations
Forgotten speech sits
on thallus and thalli, on rhizines and
refugium. I lie down where people used
to remove their shoes before entering the
temple. I reflect on the not-yet and the
long-gone, space in general, then space
between lichens. The time lag between
the sexual fruiting body and the asexual
fruiting body of every lichen
They are the future
gazing
at us
... Pattern alterers, rock weatherers,
multispecies
sculptors of non-languages —
perhaps these are their actual
names

THESE FRAGMENTS I HAVE PRESERVED

This story that must be told;
that can only be told by not telling

—M. NourbeSe Philip

all stories have silences but some can only be told with silence / sleeping on the grass my mother said you must decipher both half- and full-silences / learn to un-tongue in silence's long corridors

the silence of resistance ≠ the silence of obedience / the silence of peace ≠ the silence of desolation / sleeping she said after years of apprenticeship you will relish / also / the untold

pleasures of remaining silent / silence makes alchemy / possible / deep reflection / creation possible / sapien-ness / and sometimes amistad and love possible / listen, over there a mere survival depends on

silence / canyons of stratified silences grow / noisy with time / her index finger pointed at the silhouettes / of silence / my silence(s) / the silence(s) of others / and earth's occasional silence / sleeping on the grass my mother caressed / my brow and left for another year

AFTER A WALK IN THE RAVINE

For days now I have seen
on my kitchen island

a kabocha ripen — an entire
planet painted by some invisible

hand How lovely the celadon
stripes on depths of green

and the flowery scar
on its thick, thick skin

Tomorrow is the Mexican
día de los muertos

Numbers and sizes
of clouds and ghosts

grow   An empire is
crumbling   The young seriously

reflect on the inadequacy of old
frames for mountains, rivers and rain

and the old no longer worry
about an   awkward   hairdo

  as they find new
emotions more adequate than hope

and despair   After
the walk I climb up less filled

with disquiet   Kabocha squash in
every window

PU'ER

Bei Dao's cantos of exile suddenly made
less heavy by our host's warm Pu'er tea

Three poets read the English translation
somewhere between the mountains and the prairies

and later while taking the wrong
exit toward Edmonton's airport
Benjamin's task of the translator
also enters the evening

Exile demands quick answers
dissolves bad questions
Good questions
stay behind like tea leaves

Who am I?
What do I really want?—both
dissolve

Why will I never know who I am?
Why will I never know what I really want?—both
stay

HIMALAYAS

Sometimes my father would take me along
to the border inspections
on the Indian side — in precarious tents
jawans manned radio sets, Morse code
transmitters In double
parkas we would climb
with soldiers who knew
the terrain
like some enigmatic oral tradition

Condensed milk tea they offered
us once Their post (and makeshift kitchen)
atop a glacier and Nanga Parbat (naked
mountain) greeted us from the Pakistani side
In half-English,
half-Punjabi my father spoke to the radio
men, while I couldn't tear my eyes
away from the ancient gleam of Nanga Parbat

understanding only a phrase or two of military
language punctuated with blade sharp ACRO
NYMS All I could do there was sip
and I keep sipping that warm liquid

in the middle of the coldest war

until an adult utters a word that lies
somewhere between beauty
and ugliness: NAASH
a sudden hand tremor spilling the contents
of my childish mug onto the five-hundred-thousand-year-old
glacier

The spill long
gone, the glacier too

and as I gaze at the plastic tree at an Edmonton
airport cafe   I cannot stop
following the stoic
soldier who climbed down with us
that day He was from the deep
South   In his language only one word
                                                            for rain   fog   ice
                                                                                            and snow

how strong the wind was at that hour

bringing snow
to our faces   then taking it away

ON DAYS LIKE THIS THE PRAIRIE

On days like this I'm

convinced the prairie is a long poem
But I am not slow

enough, nor do I digress enough, and lacking
deep memory of grass, how shall I e

ven begin? Of course there's T— [long dead]
over there sitting by the steel

river   uttering how her weathered
body learned to lend an ear to grass

                                   Rivers
recount because someone's listening   she used to

say   Wind agitates sparse *grasse*
sgrassesgrasses

lifting, depositing, ungraving

the erased syllables   You must not take
them for granted those abiding meristems

those enduring echoes   of insects

preceding the sounds they make   She used
to say   walk from one circle of stones to another

from one erratic to another   Walk
from one unreconciled surface to another

and worry not if a border forms
or a border dissolves

This blue gramma has lonlonlonggg
waited to be grazed by bison   and the bison are

returning from the dead   Know that that grass
will never be fully legible   try unfurling

mashkosio kahentákon wiingaashk… Why
on days like this I feel beyond belief

our biome's ground is a closure-refusing lo
                                        ng ppooeemm?

But my testimony is not di
rect enough, my ears not intimate

enough   always failing

to conceal the lack—that deep
        ungraspable imagi   nation of grass

HÜZÜN

—a coffee reading—

On the inner wall of the cup's porcelain
two women standing
            on the shoulders
of three women standing
            on the shoulders
of seven women… Earth colours
all of them are
            wearing   hair
moving like sea kelp
            signing its name

Faint the voices   faint
            What are the women
in the cup saying, what do they keep
            saying?

Hüzün?

The Turkish word for endless melancholy
But a different mood

exists outside
the cup   Outside

with her thumb
and finger a little girl attempts to zoom

in on a rock

NO FIXED ADDRESS

—after watching a Werner Herzog documentary—

The volcano's beauty parallels the quality
of a runaway dream
What was a house in a village
now a game of mahjong
            no one plays
On a charred plate with a spoon
            cold ash particles
Cars and cattle
            drowned in fire's aftermaths
Languages with scripts
            half-evaporated
The one-way street sign has shifted too
            Tomorrow in the parking
lot a survivor will surprise the birds
            by playing again
and again the tape that recorded
            someone running after an apple

THE OTOLITH

My neighbour's granddaughter just read "The Fish"
in school   I doubt she knows the gift
she received today will make her less
lonely as a grown-up
Less lonely we three stepped inside

the store listening to her recite Elizabeth Bishop
                                                    In the frozen
food section a woman was perfectly
still   holding
up a piece of frozen salmon

Suspended in the flood
of halogen lights   from
unshrinking distance we watched the cold
in her coldening hands

Machine-cut piece of modern salmon
spawned in a farm in some far-

away place   I could not help
but think about that salmon's ear
bones, the tiny otolith
that once helped with its navigation   Stone
made of calcium carbonate, and yet
and yet

how it awakens

on the tip of a human
finger   On that TV
channel   the multi-
species anthropologist's voice-over had stressed—
          Otolith's $CaCO_3$ layers
tree-ring-like
            archive
a fish's diet, migration routes, levels of stress

The archive
always contains what it does not contain
if I have learned anything

anything so far
It was simply
too late to let that fish go   but the woman

carefully let it go among the other
frozen pieces Only then
she blinked One could almost
hear that blink Wordlessly

our six ears   paid

attention to her heels
clicking away toward the big empty
          street from where the clouds
looked stunning
reminding us of a language not yet
spoken

ROAD CLOSED

On the road to the museum the hands
of young people

glued to asphalt   At first it seemed intricate
chalk

drawings   or another powerful onion
of a slogan set up for defeat   The next instant

traffic lights
lost   usual meaning   cars   more cars

paused   On the sidewalk   shedding
my gloves   I kept walking   my first

thought not of Earth   but the wound
those hands would have to live with

when separated
from that conglomerate of human-made rock

The evening sun like some fading thappu
kept falling on silences

thousands of them inside or outside
cars, silences   inseparable from

the story that wants the road to the museum   to remain
open   forever

Heavy and frac-tured the sun

kept hardening the voices of the demonstrators   Broken meta-
carpals of light   lay on their about-to-be-broken

fingers

What I learned from them is still
warm in my hands

I felt like a six-year-old
who suddenly sees whales everywhere

whales swimming
between   asphaltpalms

Between   asphaltpalms
new species and songs   almost

ready to emerge in the half-
bruised light of this world

Forcefully a voice
repeats how inseparable we are from what we see

as separate   And when the road resumed
it was no longer the same

road   And when the museum opened
it was no longer the same museum

ELK ISLAND

I stand by an old pond
not far from six bison who have come back
          from the dead

I feel a new emotion
like the person who has just heard   microbes
          deep under us
make oxygen even in the absence of light

It is five in the afternoon
Someone else's footsteps
          approach
For a moment the shadows
of our heads merge on prairie grass

Ana says so many have come
back this summer
When the dead are passing by
the pond stops croaking

How lovely the tadpoles are
How lovely the tadpoles
we say at the same time

THE PRAIRIE

Dark again

Palimpsest grass No wind
On the country highway
Only one car

Phone rings The driver
turns

Back and as he's turning
The buffalo rubbing stone
Tries to read him in the high
beams

Dark again Voices of insects

LAWS & RIVERS

do glaciers have standing?

            do lakes, rivers, rocks, trees?

            is rain a person?

why cannot cod

and orca   go

            to our courts

            like corporations?

I break. I break bread. I
break bread with. I break
bread with Rita. I break
bread with Rita Wong

and learn from her the meaning
of beholden

RE-READING CAVAFY

Why did we melt the Hindu Kush
glaciers?
        There's no other way to deal with the Cavafians

Why do our senators call
tar sands oil sands?
        The Cavafians like it this way

Why are our best minds injecting
sulphur into the stratosphere?
        Preparations for the Cavafian arrival

Why did we not take care
of the plankton and the Atlantic?
        The Cavafians expected any time now

Rumours are spreading — the Royal
Library pulped half its collection?
        The Cavafians worship good taste

Why did our Emperor start
a new war?
        The Cavafians admire winners

Why do the major cities suddenly look extra
bright?
        The cities shine anticipating the Cavafians

CLIFFS OF DOVER

Their soft white chalk has always left him
stunned   Skeletons of coccolithophore

plankton   each particle   thin-
ner than pashmina… On the TV

channel once — how
the cliffs formed   Alive the plankton   hung out

near water's surface   Billions, centillions
must've sank down onto the sea floor

for millions of years during the warm Cretaceous
Fossil   now   all   In less than an hour

his flight will land at Gatwick No snow on that waiting
runway   The hostess still rolling trolleys and most aisles

and windows masticating microwaved cheese
buns, the treat he denied himself   Many a time he has crossed

the English Channel
by ferry   speculating   *what if*

the human voices inside the subsea cables
started mingling with the voice of water

Perhaps that's where the beginning of his long
poem is: *this body   my body*

also a part of the hydrological cycle

Voices leaking into each other   But
for now he only mutters   *So many dead*

plankton   Tries to spell co cco
lithophores with an index

finger   In the plane washroom staring
at the semi-colons of soap on mirror

he stutters   *What's my tradition? In our*
informal new epoch can one even ask?

Gurgling vacuum noises come
from the adjacent washroom

while he quits his sweater
          A rare clarity

in voice   My tradition is as old as
mountains, rivers, oceans, air, fire, the warming

lizard on stones   [These aging hands
                    and eyes ready
                    now to perform the so-
          called *late work*
                    before the dark abyss
                    of time embraces

my name]   The fluvial, the lacustrine, the aeolian — all my
traditions —   Kilimanjaro

glaciers expressing themselves, forming
moraines, meromictic lakes…Salted plastic reptating…

Foraminifera… Wind conversing with leopard's eyes… Santorini…
The Atacama desert, the cliffs of Dover, all of them

*

For five minutes he sleeps like a child, then for five
he almost cries like a child… That mid-air geologic

epiphany of his: far more
deceptive than his smartphone's Flight Path app

programmed with algorithms that erase
the peopled rafts   refugees

coming this way from some great continent
down South   *Will the anthropocene end if we stop calling it by that name?*

*

One family in those rafts

whose village was quarked
with weapons dispatched by the North then quick-

fixed by machinery bearing foreign

names Their stunning seaside "belongs"
now to a conglomerate of hotels called *Gibraltar*

or *Zermatt* He senses a cold
saline liquid rising from his failings to his brow

This human
system too,
my tradition

*

I am Bei Dao writing with glaciers exiled by the human species
I am Rita Wong protesting peacefully the Trans Mountain pipeline
I am Ó Tuama using lyric to resolve the Indus Water conflict
I am Szymborska locating the probability of bare life
in cruel statistics

I am the scientist putting sulphur in stratosphere
also the one opposed to ever putting sulphur in stratosphere

I am not that family   in the raft
and I am that family   in the raft

One family lugging

ghosts — a liminal raft it is — ghosts
of a house, a market, a square, plants,
animals, friends, of whatever was

the closest thing to a prayer

I am the berafted parent
fearing   for their daughters   sons
The wind that keeps wetting itself
The sea that keeps misreading rain's pages
I am rain

London's 33 C
air quality, etc. All clear

The pilot reminds the passengers
of the seat belt sign

He shuts his eyes and fails to shut his ears

*

Hope will come from the end of the poem

and the end of the poem will be spoken

/

by the Huachipaire of Amazon who learned Eshuva, the sung prayers, from birds

Hope will come from the end of the poem

and the end of the poem will be spoken

/

by the Temiar of Malay rain forests who were taught songs by non-humans in dreams

Hope will come from the end of the poem

and the end of the poem will be spoken

/

by the Iñupiaq of the North who received music as a gift from whales

REMAINING TIME

Mornings I go through scientific papers
on savannahs

and pampas
written by a blind person

I hear the rustle of other
languages of seeing   and want to

hear more   Evenings I compare
translations of the great eighth-century poet

from China who found a good enough
way to survive the falling

Tang empire Some afternoons
inspiration swirls me like

a gust in tallgrass prairie
                    Impels me to compose

a page or two I didn't even know
I had within me   In the remaining hours

I think of how
time itself keeps accelerating

even as I feel everything at this stage
takes twice as long to do

Last night I read Du Fu's early poem
Gazing at Mount Tai

How scantly
appreciated he was in his time

THE MAN WHO COULDN'T EAT ORANGES

Only a handful of old dark
room photographs remain
Here, my great uncle
          He's back from a long
journey   the same
conscientious face   as always a solemn wooden
bowl of fruit near his bed   That risk-

laden scent of oranges   Again and again he
          smells a Khasi
orange deep, so deep in the distempered room
nothing   else matters

All afternoon he moves
an orange from one calloused
hand to another as if it were a
spherical hymn   sometimes

loudly complaining about some billionaire's son's lavish wedding
and sometimes reclaiming the dying
art of storytelling

As I approach his age now I recall
Benjamin's storytellers   and sit
          by the kerosene lamp
          that no longer exists
trying to replicate that singular
          hypertender way
the man in the photograph touched the forbidden
fruit   Doctor's orders   All

the rivers in his stories
have changed courses   and trees have migrated
Only what he held in his hands
remains   Once I picked up

          the rolling
dropped orange
          and he bowed
saying over and over ra'ab ter'a bha'la kar'e
ra'ab bha'la kar'e   ra'ab ter'a bha'la kar'e
as if I had just given him back
          his breath

MOTHER

The language whose last speaker just passed
on

is how I experience   The afternoon sun of my adopted
city   The metallic fountain for horses

Mother in a
dream washes my hands and in the icy square a palash
                                        blooms

LAUGHTER

—for Eden Robinson—

The bus journey to the high mountains
less tiring

This time I found myself sitting next to
three monks

Staying at the cheapest inn
and having just stepped out to buy a cake

of soap   I will walk tomorrow to
upper Dharamshala — an interview

at the Tibetan Children's Village
If they select me I will teach

physics   Grades ten and eleven
Not clear if I will get to see

the claret-robed lama this time
I have travelled long to be

near the lama's marvellous laughter
Don't even understand   why

all these years it roomed
as a compulsory mineral in my gut

It is saying   we are free
to laugh anytime   anywhere

I am telling Eden Robinson
about the laughter

Her laughter is reminding me
of that laughter so long ago

AFTER MY DEFEAT

After my defeat   reparations followed
Migrating caribou
                        changed course
A million glowing tracks
in dense katabatic wind   In
                            earthbreath
I was the caribou   and I was
the ears of the lichen-rock they licked

GRASS MUST HAVE GROWN BY NOW

What if the one shaving in front of the mirror
says my utterance is
not modern   not modern

enough?

*

I move away from the good manners
of poetry, name

the storm

*

A woman carrying a bag of autumn
leaves crosses
the street, moves further and further
away from the church
yard she just cleaned
She is wearing
stories no one notices   Only the little
child who says "yellow" "yellow"
                                    "red" "red"

*

The air's broken. The air's pure
shard

The air's no longer able to watch Matthew Wong
paint

The air's no longer able to offer space
to his birches

Who has broken it? Why break
what's already broken?

You [over there] whose hands
repair   I'd love to offer you salal

*

She asks, What if the whole city
reincarnates?

Stalactites have grown in my eyes, I say

*

The poetry of the Anthropocene
includes the Pentagon

the Chinese, the Indian
the Russian, the Israeli

militaries   Add the British
the Koreans

France, Iran, Pakistan, Germany,
Saudi…

Deep Time— the sole informer

Again ripples in my bathtub
Again F-16s are passing by

*

Grass must have grown by now
in the oil refinery

*

She notices clothes floating in the sea

She runs asking where
are the women? men?
children?

In the gallery
workers hang Matthew
Wong's *Dialogue*

Wong's "white"
the white
of an unpainted canvas

*

The drummer by the metro
station   puts the frame
drum aside
and steels
her own body
to make music The drum-
mer becomes the drum

*

I had prayed to the goddess Give me
                                        solitude
Give me hands that can drink proverbs
from fountains of grass

I had not asked her for loneliness
                    the Siamese twin
of solitude   Past midnight now
I stretch a rubber band between my lips

They grow warm   Stay
warm till the wee hours
of our epoch's day voices

TRAIN JOURNEY

In the glass between him and the passing world
he studies major & minor

catastrophes   Snow on his face and three lines
composed by a contemporary whose name for some

reason keeps slipping   away
On sand / the old man stands / in his father's skates

He knows there's at least one other
person somewhere who's thinking

the same   He puts drops
in his drying eyes   drinks the remaining

carajillo   Strange
sunset!   Aramaic clouds   Flamingoes

AFTER 40 YEARS[1]

In Trilokpuri again the little girl waves
her hand

listens to stones slicing
the wind

She goes near very near
trees that are comforting the grass

Closely she reads water-
marked history books translating
traces of bullet-holes in Jallianwalah Bagh
while the traces
mourn also the dead of 1984

Don't say we've no memorial
Don't say we've no memorials

In Trilokpuri again the little girl waves
her hand and the wave

is our memorial

—2024

1 November pogroms, India

THINGS I MISS

after dying—

smell of nutmeg
words such as *saudade*, a smile, listening
to the composer
Einaudi's elegies
for the arctic, washing an apple
in a cold stream, sleeping
on a forbidden question, and the habit
that had unknowingly become mine   of seeing

the Buddha even in uncarved rock

OPPENHEIMER

He sees Nevada-
sized mushrooms   Fire
nibbling a bride's dress He sees cities

forgetting their own names
It isn't that
            I don't feel

bad. It's that I don't
feel worse
tonight than I did last night

Again rain begins falling
where it should

and should not
and should never

INUKSHUKS

I.

people continue to disappear
on their own or
Ice makes them disappear

II.

from Latin
disappearance
to cease, vanish

III.

Again in the playground the little girl
is waiting for the little boy
What will happen now? Their
grand plan
to inukshuk?

She
gathers and stacks up stones
makes her inukshuk
But already

her mother wants
her back home

gathering
more
stones
she makes a second one on behalf of the no-show

then runs toward
her mother's
splintering   silhouette

From some
distance I compare them
Not the first

but the second
inukshuk
glows

IV.

Until I disappear

on behalf of the disappeared
Will I make inukshuks?

COMPLETENESS

Darwish isn't born yet

Darwish will be born
when two leaves sprout

One real
One imagined — more

effulgent   Right now

how complete
the night is

DARWISH

By the Pacific Ocean   a grand
university campus

I look up—

Cherry blossoms
urge every *stone to bloom*

I look down—

On asphalt the student protestors
have left behind words in chalk

Two local poets strolling along
                yes,

the Great Dane still
makes perfect coffee

Why this hesitation?

I cannot tear myself apart
from the melancholy asphalt

those sticky chalk words
The protestors are headed

now toward the darkening glass
library   Foghorn

sounds follow them
and so many rub

their eyes   I don't know
if they too heard the footsteps

of the ghost
of Darwish

Under a cherry tree   he planted
himself

witnessing history
No idea if the students

reread   *where should the birds fly after*
the last sky

when later that night each one was alone
in a room   I did

BRASSO

Childhood, always a mountain town
I am a school

boy in my father's
regimental office that afternoon—

walnut desk, a provocative red lamp, an ink pot, a pile
of khaki files, shining

name plate, the door handle
smell of Brasso—

when an unannounced soldier
walks in—tall, clean-shaven—a telegram

having informed him moments ago
that back home a beloved has passed

Father stands up
from the swivel chair   takes a few steps

puts a hand on the bestilled man's shoulder
says a ten-day leave will be sanctioned

said it with such affection   the kind
he had held back   from me

and perhaps   from the rest
of the fluxing world

I sat like a statue
on a three-legged stool

unaware of silence's power   and that
of words, gestures,

the shining-Brasso-cleaned
objects in the office, how some day they would begin

interrupting my everyday
                                        and now   I know

I must make time for the long reach
of things gazing from the past

EVERY YEAR

During my father's visits we
sit in cafes where one can talk limit
lessly about the size & the type
of sugar cubes while dropping
them in small bitter cups

With the forceps
of his thumb and index finger
my father holds a cube

and before letting it fall
always he brings the cube's lower surface
in contact
with the upper surface of the dark
brimming liquid

With great pleasure he watches
that coffee being wicked up
until the cube
just about begins
to disintegrate in the shaking

hand
Some cubes last longer
Both of us love the cubes
that last longer

IDENTITY

Sometimes I feel
I have none

Or so many—

Yesterday it seemed
a crowd

almost   Each one

with a sharp shadow
Each

one
tense, behaving

like a potter
who has lost faith

in clay
and doesn't know it yet

WINTER SOLSTICE

I.

Weather is stochastic,
but climate presents a
fastidious rhythm   Erosion's
got no rhythm, but formation
of average sedimentary
rock   clearly marked
with rhythm This is all I
thought this morning walking in falling
snow

II.

Afternoon, the usual cup of flat
white On the foam the barista's
tulip

III.

In the evening
I noticed a dimly glowing
stranger with a black dog
            walking and stopping
            walking and stopping
and I felt walking   with someone
may or may not establish a rhythm

I remembered
the trace and aura
of a dream Walking with Borges
climate modellers asking him
the meaning of *Del Rigor En La Ciencia*
                The storyteller's silence
emitting   the scent of time
His shadow in some strange metamorphic hurry
although it was white
everywhere and no one was
waiting

INTERROGATE ME

The dam
aged North

Saskatche
wan river

just south of the old tower where I rent an apart
ment Short
winter days already
I don't have a car
So when Mr. W demanded my parking
spot I offered it right away

a Mongolian poet
he left outside my door
settling the debt

Ochirbatyn Dashbalbar's *Grass Trilogy*
diminished melancholia
at once lowered and lifted
my head But something else
went amiss One building resident

the cops said "disappeared"
Cleaners stumbled upon a stash of hand-
written pages on his floor I borrowed
one—

Pick up the debris
of light   Un-music
*   sounds like music*

By the church
entrance he will stop
*   reciting the wasteland*

Everyone an underground
poet now   Who said
our mouth-made sounds have the right
to last?

Cabbages grow
out of R.K.'s ears

Either I'm dreaming
*   or a madman*
*   The mad always*
*   deny*
*   madness   So what*
*   am I…*

Perhaps I am in the middle

…Do not just freeze on the scrolls
of North Saskatchewan… Interrogate me,
Poetry

In snow-lit dark
my solitude accumulates   I bookmark
Ochirbatyn Dashbalbar's
trilogy with traces
of the disappeared man

Interrogate me,
Poetry

THE OLD MASTER'S LAST INTERVIEW

Never draw rain as dotted lines, I will tell my younger self. Neither my art teacher nor my science prof ever corrected me when I painted a tear drop and called it rain. The shape of rain is spherical (when the drops are really small) or like the upper bun of a hamburger (when not so small). The bun grows, shape-shifts into a fragile parachute before exploding into thousands of smaller spheres. Time itself ruptures. Let me make my own mistakes, my younger self tells me. Let me imagine a world different from our world

THE SCALE OF A POEM

—la poesía es la esperanza de lo que no tiene esperanza—

For instance at the breakfast
table   eating overnight oats

we could have appreciated
those who write

on a single grain of rice
or the ones who desire writing inside

a single neuron   but the storm
winds carried us toward Chile   Zurita?

                                                  you said—where's Raúl Zurita?

Months go past
Neither one of us has any clue
Zurita is busy dancing with
            the earth
            The tremor in hands
he calls beautiful—
someone writes to us

a saint and a sinner
don't leave him

alone   But where is

he?   Z's persuading *la gente* to walk
in knee-deep saltwater   interpret
translations of his work on sinking

child refugees

At night he beams words onto cliffs
Listens to gusts (un)
stitching histories

Real hard work it is
convincing the dead   They
still believe "Pinochet's alive"

All humans are walking-talking minerals
Zurita is   a dancing rock

Two electric hands turn and turn on earth-moving gadgets & condensation-
trailing

aircraft   Flying

over a maximum city he's sky writing

With bulldozers Zurita is growing
the alphabet in the Atacama Desert

We hear Z's going to earth-write the longest poem ever written

and he does

From the window seat
of a plane we read
the complete
three-mile-long poem

Ni pena Ni miedo

Only four words long   the longest poem

Without pain or fear

and there and there Zurita is
in the middle of the Atacama
uttering   hoping   dancing

THE SEA IS HISTORY

An early twenty-first century colour

photo of you in a half-ironed cyan shirt almost
sitting at the feet

of the visiting myth
Walcott

whispered in your ear right
after the photographers drowned in the

minor infinity of the crowd
No small

talk, but a little torque,
jokes, belly laughter, the habitat

of egrets before he too
disappeared in hexameter's paintbrush

and prodigal waves

That night the moon
moved an inch closer to earth

MORNING QUESTIONS

On my face grandmother
sprinkles water
This will invite   good
spirits   keep bad ones
away   Where are you now,

water? Where have you gone?

THE RUNWAY

An intercontinental plane has landed
It's still on the runway
The woman inside looks out
Mild rain
People's phones
pinging again A miracle, almost
three infants on board
and not a single one cried Slanted
drops roll down
the glass Suddenly a feeling —
she's not looking at the falling
rain   The rain's looking
at me   at us
she says to herself with a light smile
Soak us, rain, with your language
Teach us the middle voice of the verb

HIDDEN AGENDA

Just for memory's
sake   can I keep one icicle,
Sun?

Just like a candle
lights other candles
I will use this one icicle, make

glaciers

GO SLOW

—a lookout in Banff—

Out of diminishing fog

Hoodoos emerge

Sometimes erosion is not
the interruption in rhythm,

erosion is
the rhythm
Let us imagine

geologic gods
exist and they assemble
more-than-human
ensembles
of toy performers, a standing
open-
air orchestra—
drums, wind, pinnacles of palaeo
stone instruments (scaled-up)   each Hoodoo
a singular timbre—

Wait
I can even hear faint staccatos
and legatos
of an unfamiliar gamelan
This composition
remembers to follow

no plot   abraids out of the half-
written score—completes

the circle   Each
hoo-
doo
alive in some aeolian gap
between the colloidal small
and a Chomolungma
mountain

I hear big gongs, layers
of time
within time   Time listening
to time?

Shall I go near, touch the standing waves?
Change the pulse of the turning
Earth?

At
this lookout
numerous other
eyes
and ears, each one awed
in their own way   a diversity

of astonishments

On my left   the crouching person
keen only on hearing
                the grass
near her sandals
as a bee crawls
out of an aster
On sadness' threshold
she utters *Some bloom*
to mark the be-
ginning of the end of summer

Sitting in half-lotus posture
the stranger on my right
could as well perform   or replace
my grandfather [O that wheezing
breath]

this place as if a bird about to emerge
from the pages of Nanak

[and the choric
                voice — the ocean's wandering
bottom—yearning to become sky again]

Near the last hoodoo   a half-buried wood-
en bench
Buried by the floodwaters in 2013
—the year my mother was freshly

dead Sometimes she sits   on that
bench
Vowels she loves more now
than consonants *Say oo'doo*
                                  Say oo'doo
I don't know if she faces   this
way or that

The pages of her favourite book open and shut
Their shadows open and shut

alongside   The bird's already
slowly beating its widening
wings
                Where now?

Shall I delete the beginning of every note?
Preserve only the ends?

Prolong the diminuendos?

Go slow
Eroding bird

Go slow
Eroding gamelan

BONE DENSITY

Today [he promises himself] he'll not compare
his interior with the diminishing corals
The caring person who just prepared his body
for the scan wants him to be more
still than he is. Only his mind can
move now. He hears his sister
the positive thinking she recom-
mends   The scan has started
He shuts his eyes   is surrounded
by seagrass. Oxygen rise
              s from the b
              lades of sea
grass Little bell sounds he'd heard
in a shrine when he was five
You may go to the change room now
He's sure the person who just scanned
will not share the alarming numbers. (Over
the years a helpful little trick)
Observe like some Malmö detective   the tone
of their voice   the facial
expression when they utter
You'll find out everything from the doctor later
But this time it is different. He asks
no question. Only smiles
as he exits the room. He wants the little
bells to continue ringing a bit
longer within the highs and lows
of his bones

ARE THE SCALLOP'S EYES FOR REAL?

a child asks
How could I answer her So little
I know about eyes let alone a scallop's telescopic vision

Dōgen suggests befriending
and moving from ego to eco   intimacy
with all things   I guess that's what I'll tell her
Look, the scallop's gaze is resting

on us   and it's also resting on the seagrass
Listen, we are lucky, the seagrass is still voicing
something to the scallop
just like it's still voicing something to me and you

THE TRANSLATOR'S HOME

Memory   the heaviest piece
of furniture

Small tasselled
carpet, symmetrical birds,

foliage   Lemon, mint,
smell of caraway crackling

Half-open window
Outside's cold road

visible   Inside, warm
like the Mediterranean

The soul? Two shrines
take care of it

The book and
the turntable

Look at the stripping
wall paint

Even the amlas
in the fridge suggest

in-betweenness is the rule
here   not the exception

IF OIL COULD SPEAK

In the shade of elms
he would sit and feed small town pigeons break-
fast   muttering ruins
& proverbs   They say

he'd arrived here right
after the newspapers started calling
South-East Kakania ex-
South-East Kakania

Over a million necklaces memory makes
me wear   Migration—
            the most twisted necklace

His jokes—always
off, objectionable, but
they gave him away
more than his other sayings
                The only violence over here
occurs   when in the dark a person
imagines a hungry lynx   a polar bear

He missed that minor
            monument
of a personal library
back home The complete
Works of Thomas Bernhard

Januaries-Februaries we would stroll
to our city's glacial erratics together
There he would try on me
many possible endings
for the pieces he was contemplating
          abandoning

Endings didn't come
easy The essay
"Gasoline Alley"
will always remain

unfinished   The first real turn
in his small press life—
Compile the lit. history of coal
     Dense, breathless

passages, most people were drawn
to unpolished gems
"If oil could speak
what would it say?"

I am losing my words
some of us heard from May
till November
and then he lost them

"If oil could speak what would it say?"

"But are we listening?"

OUT IN THE OPEN

Abandoned poem, you will
hang outside my door
next to the horseshoe

DOS NACIMIENTOS

coinciden
el nacimiento del agua
y el nacimiento de la poesía

por la caída peligrosa

cuando recuerdo
esto un poco
de mi inquietud

se disuelve

La mitad de mi vida se ha ido / analizando grandes conjuntos de datos / de calidad de agua / turbiedad / transparencia / oxígeno disuelto / amoníaco / cadmio / mercurio / a las cinco / después de terminar el trabajo / en el lab de arenas bituminosas / caminé a casa a lo largo / del río sensible / la ciudad / estaba perdiendo su brillo / los abedules ocupados / contabilizándo / las hojas / que habían perdido / cerca del banco del parque / escuché a alguien / y sentí / que te estaba escuchando / "Much of Earth's water is older / than the Earth / even older / than the Sun / Look, the moon tonight will be as viscous as remembering" /

TWO BIRTHS

coincide
the birth of water
and the birth of poetry

by the caída peligrosa

when I recall
this a little
of my disquiet

dissolves

Half my life has gone / analyzing large data sets / of water quality / turbidity / transparency / dissolved oxygen / ammonia / cadmium / mercury / at 5 / after finishing work / at the oil sands monitoring lab / I walked home along / the sentient river / the city / was losing its brightness / the birches occupied / accounting / the leaves / they had lost / near the park bench / I heard someone / & felt / I was hearing you / "Much of Earth's water is older / than the Earth / even older / than the Sun / Look, the moon tonight will be as viscous as remembering" /

PACIFIC SPIRIT

—Wreck beach, Vancouver—

All day it has rained
and all this wetness has moved
me unword-ward

Carrying an intermittent umbrella
I stumble into a littoral place
I cannot read and I do not want to

But here too
the city follows
A distant car comes to a screeching
halt   impacts something

"Ecology is
prepositions," my friend
had announced. "I am done with thinking

about water"

What did she mean?

Walking
then standing on these well-
rounded pebbles   I struggle
to attend the masterclass

of water The master-

class of water
the deep voice of a translator
for whom nothing is foreign
Curious, how it reads

a surface?
a depth?
a secret?

a loss?

I want to learn how to read *with*
water
Near me rain

lingers a little
longer on the bark of a cedar
and that shivering gull's slow walk
is still

remembered
by the wave that came
before this wave

MINOR PERTURBATIONS

I. KITCHEN WINDOW

A tree and a bird
    It and *it* —
the limits of my language

II. ONE-PAW CLAPPING

Buddha's birthday
The dog says time
For our walk

III. TELL ME LIES

Greenland ice is growing
Gr enland ice s gro ing

EARTH TIDES

I.

The planet is not as rigid as we
originally surmised
the field notes say

Near the centre of a million-person city
an earth scientist knows it rises
every night by more than a foot

once again she cannot stop
thinking about land tides
the way some can
not stop thinking about sea tides

With a fingertip she touches a tiny
bee on the kitchen floor
Did someone move the garbage bin
again?

Waves of the unanswerable
rise and ebb within her — what was the shape
& the size of land waves
when a few billion years ago the moon was a whole
lot closer to earth? What exactly
was the meaning
of catastrophe then? Beauty?

Everything is stretchable   The rock
beneath us not as rigid as we
originally surmised

Slowly the city is
falling   Tonight she can almost feel
            the earth-crust,
pushing, pulling… Her partner
glued to Bob Marley
In the attic   both
daughters fast asleep but she still

cannot let the one bee   in her hand   go

II.

The bee
makes her drift again   she spec-
ulates the illegible wind that leaked it

in here   The bee
makes her more
aware of the beats
of the new un-compostable epoch
          a hive drips
into her ear

Bees dream
she read in *Nature* last fort-
night What are they

like?   Bees dream
This is all we know

all we can ever know

MILK

This Thursday night
History is being made

In the corner store
A man is buying milk

In the kitchen he is
drinking it   now he is

washing the bowl   Milk &
soap are altering the planetary

phosphorus cycle Like me,
and you, he, too,

forgot the turning Earth

Blessed are night thoughts
that end like this

Sometimes they want me
to go look for the milk carton,

the grass and the cow as well
My insomnia listens to that now

familiar choric voice — Everything is a king
and a queen   making history

NIGHT

Walk at night   the facilitator says
Walk so silently until the bottoms of your feet become ears

Walking we hear low tones
of clay   Slumps,

shakes of a carnivorous flower
Mutterings,

convulsions of a broken tooth
We hear frost building up

on a lost wedding ring
Faint shouts of a dung beetle

Persistence of a lemon-seed flute
Birth pangs of a new rare-earth

element a million years in advance

The bottoms of our feet
hear language   flowing in an aquifer's dreams

We hear a stone questioning
                                        our idea of immortality

NIGHTS

                    Cities so bright
Taxis floating in rivers   of light
Darkness summons me from childhood's
words and roof
terraces Somewhere between
Ludhiana & Amritsar
my grandparents and I are asleep
with stars about to land on us   a constellation
falls on our jute cots   our embryo bodies

Cities so bright, the brightness of boulevards and office towers
Bridges blink
mutilated and mutilating wavelengths
In this dark I feel home-
sick for that dark

and O my love how can I forget
Valencia   the last stages
of its dusks
Valencia where I failed to figure out
the gender
of "oscuridad" and of "luz"
and you had come toward me with open
arms and said both are

feminine   Your language

and your tongue I have
preserved so carefully all
these years   and what you whispered
later about binaries

Together we stayed until
the last fingers of darkness
came out of asphalt and were plucked by light

EARTH COMES IN

again Earth revolves the turnstiles
comes in through our doors

acoustic ghosts   untold numbers
                              wander everywhere
                              and appoint hearers

fish can no longer be fish
grass no longer grass
even a hearer can
no longer be a proper hearer

what shall I not do?
and what shall I do?

again the inexplicable happens
again Earth comes in through our doors

THE GATELESS GATE

From the bathtub   you
halt me with
Earth was
already in
here   the turnstile
                                        too is the Earth

I AM NOT THE SALMON / I AM THE SALMON

Sitting by what remains
of the river   thought begins

to move   Water language
leaks into the whole

range of my verbs   Thirty-five
years ago feels like yesterday when I went to sleep

under a camphor and woke up under a douglas fir

Within days of arrival that current-
within-a-current of a voice
        conjugated
my ribs and spoke about the land   my body
had just borrowed

It is different
The voice said
Different   to be
With a place
When one calls it
The place
Where salmon gather

Running up
salmon were making radical water
murals
Murals that remember
the Great Acceleration
as a million years away
and as a million years behind

And may some flickering street-
lamp fully figure out why
nouns trouble
me from that moment on, why the settler's map

slipped out of my rucksack slowly
weathering on drying asphalt British

Columbia, the map said, McLennan
river, Fraser, and

all along the unwavering

voice kept coming from some
funnel somewhere
and is stronger now
within me than it was then

UNCONFORMITIES

Am I trying to write my anxieties down into the deep of the paper?

—Rosemarie Waldrop

Again comes the hour when one is not
          sure if darkness is
raising its heels to look at light or light
is standing on tiptoes investigating
darkness. Once you called such
moments ideal to take the pulse
of earth-sky. We spent
          I repeat we
spent a lifetime formulating what we thought
were good questions, but now at the onset
of dementia you often embrace stillness, silences
          or stop
in mid-thought. *Ediacarans are a good—*
          "a good example" did you mean? Often I
fail to interpret; no gesture, you
stare as if I were some dead come
back for their things. But there are moments, moments I
feel the *Ediacarans* so amply convey
you are once again immersed in deep
          time. Watching
you garden last evening I felt—the young woman was
still intact inside you, still speculating about this planet

during its earlier years. Last
night when you fell asleep I read again the doctor's
tight handwriting, how all onsets are both
unique and non-unique, and for some unknown reason I
recalled your final talk on the history of mountain
ranges, the one that received a ten-minute standing
ovation. A petro-geologist, you'd just changed your
mind about the environment. "I see only the beautiful
now that I have only one eye." All your sayings sprang
up, and how I used to agree with you each
time you questioned the use of the word *dirt*
for *earth* in the language both of us had adopted
                                        Tomorrow when we go
for our short walk in the morning, not expecting an
answer I might ask if you still recognize those two
words, and if not, what sounds have replaced them

THE EPOCH THAT DIDN'T BEGIN WITH A QUESTION

Saints used to walk
here, now we gather
soil samples

Saints used to breathe
here, now we measure air
quality

Cry silently at unframed
virtual exhibitions   the scrolling
Burtynskys

Look behind the screen
Taneda Santōka would have said
The stone / drenched with rain / points the way

PLACES

Time is an overflowing river
in India   History no

longer hesitates
here Drying

stepwells — not the only places

preferred by ghosts
Schoolchildren still

singing the morning prayer
Tamaso ma jyotir gamaya

A voice says the game
of chess was invented here   over here

Return is a wound
they had always warned you of

I look at the ruins of air
I enter the ruins of water

LAC LA BICHE DIARIES

I.

The mirrors
of Lac La Biche appear
full today Some-
one is unknitting
what they knit hours
ago

I look at the
horizon The man on the kayak
enters the frame
and departs
the frame Even the boreal
forest is sailing away

I plant a seed
Words
come out
of earth like palms
of my hands

II.

(wind direction)

↖

↖

→

III.

CBC voices: even
the finest fire-fighters
in the dry mountain
town had to flee
No idea how

safe my friends are   Only five

hours away from
each other and here too
the ash-smoke thickens
So dense is the air
with failed words,
treatises, treaties

IV.

Earth, your ever
fermenting voice—
                    the grapes we'll drink
                                        years later

V.

My mother's braiding
my hair with the epoch

I see bitumen

everywhere   Slip
into the deep well

of a Punjabi primer   There too
          cretaceous' traces

2 am: through the middle of the forest
I run like some painter
hurrying to her studio   The fossil
drawing on her
new canvas still lacks the correct gleam of dark

VI.

She says she can't
live without volcanoes He says
he'd love to die on
some pyroclastic edge

Earth-hand keeps   opening
more than a window

VII.

Who is a person? Is a lake a person?
Shall I sign

            the petition?

VIII.

and that summer we found
plastic in the thirteen-hundred-
year-old foreign-
language poem
we were translating

not an error, you said
not an error, I said
then louder together
as if for inhabitants of the future

ix.

I wake up   ask Ma
why the Kanchenjunga looks

blue   *Faraway things bluen*

Is the sky doubt-
lessly blue? My father   nods

yes and no   Is that why
I always leave the sky

unpainted?   Years pass
Looking down a well

holding a mirror   he can see now

the sky
and a picture

of that very sky
at the same time

x.

I sign the petition

XI.

Creatures crawling
on tense water, my teachers

Soon dice will fall,
Earth will win

XII.

Cyanobacteria advisory

Two-hour vipassana

The Phanerozoic flashes by
Will I finally be able to talk to all the eons
when I am gone?

Why not
        try right now?

Oxygen, don't change your amount in air
I'll not chop the wood
I'll not make fire
Stay modern, Oxygen,
as in the system scientists' *modern atmosphere*

XIII.

Night's an impasto
exclamation mark
The bench in the Matthew Wong canvas
                                        is Matthew Wong

XIV.

The vase of my loss and gain
drops from my hand
Beautiful

the shards   Wapiti,
the foreign word the little boy had learned in India
returns   His great uncle in the air force
piloted a Wapiti

And now in the snowish town
of Lac La Biche   an elk
family stands on the sidewalk
gazing at my tracks

XV.

Later news will be heard
Wâwâskesiwisâkahikan halted
The machine that invented
Words like human and animal

XVI.

Curlews
Returning
Departing

XVII.

Gales moil
almost tear the lost cat
              in the poster
glued to the electric pole
by the precarious stop

sign   Everyday more
and more I
resemble that lost Ricardo
Like Pessoa I too hold onto the liminal
heteronyms One hundred and three
                        so far and counting

XVIII.

a micro-biome in human gut
a micro-biome in fish brain

soon biologists might locate
a micro-biome in human brain

EverythingChange
un-mantles our permanent collections

our dictionary entries *Person?*

XIX.

Sirens going past
the Tim Hortons say
berries still exist
bears still exist
oil sands still exist, oil sands still exist

xx.

my friend, here I am
journeying back to the red canoes
of your childhood, the "high-
way of ice", how in those old cryo-
genic Alberta winters
car tyres fluently acquired
the shape
of a square

Still unable to draw our last
meeting: we were circumambulating
precarity — the epoch-marking
meromictic lake
in Ontario and again and again
            your pulse
            seesawed

Lac La Biche—
Your father still
a vibration
drilling holes there [here] in austere ice, your brother busy white-
fish grilling   one by one the caribou pass

Where are you now?

Does your ear-bone
still elect to run
from whatever sounds like
or names itself

a poem? Know that
only silence comes
            to me these days   sometimes
                                        accompanied by little dry waves
                                                                        of grief

NOT SOLASTALGIA

Not solastalgia
but a caesura
as if one were living in some   caesura

Not solastalgia but a line
break as if one has become a hesitation
between sound
and meaning

Not solastalgia
but stanzas
awakening to long
sounds and the aeolian

Not solastalgia
but the entangledness
of the angel of history
and the angel of geo-history

Not solastalgia
but the gap
between the atmosphere of weather
and the atmosphere of climate

Not solastalgia
but the struggle to breathe
in and out the lyric the anti-
lyric that's habitable

STILL ASTONISHED

Yes, I am still around
astonished

by those migrating monarchs   turning
and turning again on the way to Michoacán

Lasting accuracy
lives within them   a double clock   Monarchs

read the sun   maps
passed down by ancestors

Astonished

my faculties still allow me to be with
one of them before it sets out

on a long journey from the withering
habitat   I could never give a name to

DECOLONIZED LOVE

My love let us
from time to time also bring to mind the other

diamonds
not just the ones the empire stole

Like this diamond
that rose some 564 kilometres

from deep Earth
to greet us all on

the crust Within its 3-millimetre
body the diamond

carried a tiny fragment
of a mineral that just

revealed there's water
the size of three oceans

deep inside the largely
unattainable Earth

Diamonds that bring such
astonishments are rare

and not forever
but the astonishments are, my love

THE NINETY-YEAR-OLD POET RESPONDS

Strange choice you give me—
Put it all down   *Or*
leave it all out

In my poems   my friends
at once I
leave it all out and put it

all down Yet Mandelstam's
question remains   My epoch

how will I look you

in the eye

NOTES

ix: This book's first epigraph comes from Czesław Miłosz's "Bypassing Rue Descartes." *Selected and Last Poems 1931–2004* (ECCO, 2011).

ix: The second epigraph comes from Anna Tsing's "Unruly Edges: Mushrooms as Companion Species," *Environmental Humanities* 1 (1) (Duke University Press, 2012).

ix: The third epigraph comes from Tim Ingold's *Being Alive* (Routledge, 2011).

DARKNESS—
4: "What is water in the eyes of water?" comes from Alice Oswald's *Nobody: A Rhapsody to Homer* (WW Norton, 2020).

THESE FRAGMENTS I HAVE PRESERVED—
13: M. NourbeSe Philip's *Zong!* (Invisible, 2023)

ON DAYS LIKE THIS THE PRAIRIE—
18: Parts of the poem are in conversation with Layli Long Soldier's Whereas (Graywolf, 2017). *Now /Make room in the mouth / For grassesgrassesgrasses*

NO FIXED ADDRESS—
21: Werner Herzog's documentary. *The Fire Within: A Requiem for Katia and Maurice Krafft* (2022).

THE OTOLITH—
23: Heather Anne Swanson's *Spawning Modern Fish* (University of Washington Press, 2022).

LAWS & RIVERS—

28: Poet-scholar Rita Wong was sentenced to 28 days in prison for participating in a protest opposing the Trans Mountain pipeline. See also *Current, Climate* (Wilfred Laurier University Press, 2021).

THE CLIFFS OF DOVER—

32: The historian David Van Reybrouck: "There is more to colonialism than historical colonialism… Today's climate change is deeply colonial: it has largely been caused by temperate zones from the northern hemisphere and it is most deeply felt in the tropics and the Arctic. You can't decolonize without decarbonizing and vice versa."

THE MAN WHO COULD NOT EAT ORANGES—

38: See "The Handkerchief" in Walter Benjamin's *The Storyteller Essays* (2019)

GRASS MUST HAVE GROWN BY NOW—

43: See Matthew Wong, *Vincent van Gogh: Painting as a Last Resort* (Van Gogh Museum, 2024).

DARWISH—

55: *Time for stone to bloom:* Paul Celan's "Corona."
See also Mahmoud Darwish's "The Earth is Closing in Us": *where should the birds fly after / the last sky*

WINTER SOLSTICE—

61: Kyle Barnes' "On Exactitude in Climate Science," *Long Now*, February 7, 2024. See also Byung-Chul Han's *The Scent of Time: A Philosophical Essay on the Art of Lingering* (Polity, 2017). Translated from German by Daniel Steuer.

THE SCALE OF A POEM—

67: *la poesía es la esperanza de lo que no tiene esperanza / poetry is the hope of what has no hope.* See Raúl Zurita's conversation with Forrest Gander about the book *Pinholes in the Night: Essential Poems from Latin America* (Copper Canyon, 2014).

TWO BIRTHS AND DOS NACIMIENTOS—
84–85: *The Guardian*, 25 Jan, 2024: "Canadian tar sands pollution is up to 6300% higher than reported, study finds". See Matthew Wong's poem "Vincent" in Matthew Wong, *Vincent van Gogh: Painting as a Last Resort* (Van Gogh Museum, 2024).

NIGHT—
93: The lines in italics come from Pauline Oliveros' *Deep Listening: Software for People* (Baltimore, 1984).

THE EPOCH THAT DIDN'T BEGIN WITH A QUESTION—
102: Taneda Santōka. The original haiku: *Shitodo ni nurete kore wa michishirube no ishi*

PLACES—
103: *Tamaso ma jyotir gamaya... lead me from darkness to light.* From the Brihadaranyaka Upanishad.

LAC LA BICHE—
112: *apricot trees exist, apricot trees exist.* See Inger Christensen's alphabet (New Directions, 2001)

NOT SOLASTALGIA—
115: The neologism coined by the philosopher Glenn Albrecht. See also William Watkin's *The Literary Agamben* (Bloomsbury, 2010).

THE NINETY-YEAR-OLD POET RESPONDS—
118: Bronwen Tate. *Putting it all down, Leaving it all out.* (PhD Dissertation, Stanford University, 2014).

ACKNOWLEDGEMENTS

First versions of some poems appeared elsewhere: 'Completeness' in *carte blanche* #52 (2025). 'Lichen' in the inaugural issue of *Orbital Studies* (2026). 'Milk' in *World Literature Today* (July, 2026). 'Elk Island' in *Beyond the Concert Hall* (Laberinto Press, 2026). 'The Ninety-Year-Old Poet Responds', 'The Otolith', and 'Darkness' in the chapbook *Otolith* (Agatha Press, 2026). 'The Translator's Home' in *Alberta Views* (December 2025).

For known and unknown reasons I would like to thank Laurie Graham, Helmut Weissert, Julie Robinson, Natania Rosenfeld, Kim Nekarda, Derek Pardue, Iman Mersal, Malcolm Lim, Laurie Ricou, Emma Cunliffe, Rita Wong, Anne McLean, Stephen Hunt, Leilei Chen, Raji Soni, Daphne Marlatt, Bronwen Tate, *Stop.gap*, Christine Hassay-Kohler, Anton Kirchhofer, Tanya Handa, Matt Bowes, and Meredith Thompson. I am grateful to Green College (UBC) and Alberta Foundation for the Arts.

"Road Closed" is for Kim Nekarda. "The Otolith" is for Heather Swanson. "Hüzün" is for Iman Mersal. "Elk Island" is for Julie Robinson. "Darkness" is for Derek Pardue. "Winter Dialogues" is for Caleb Kan and Helmut Weissert. "Nights" is for Ana Soto. The last fragment of "Lac La Biche Diaries" is in memory of Terry Maccagno.

crow said

In 2017, to honour NeWest Press' 40th anniversary, we inaugurated a new poetry series to go alongside our Nunatak First Fiction, Prairie Play, and Writer as Critic series: Crow Said Poetry. Crow Said is named in honour of Robert Kroetsch's foundational 1977 novel *What The Crow Said*. The series aims to shed light on places and people outside of the literary mainstream. It is our intention that the poets featured in this series will continue Robert Kroetsch's literary tradition of innovation, interrogation, and generosity of spirit.

CROW SAID POETRY TITLES AVAILABLE FROM NEWEST

Tar Swan — David Martin
That Light Feeling Under Your Feet — Kayla Geitzler
Paper Caskets — Emilia Danielewska
let us not think of them as barbarians — Peter Midgley
Lullabies in the Real World — Meredith Quartermain
The Response of Weeds: A Misplacement of Black Poetry on the Prairies — Bertrand Bickersteth
Coconut — Nisha Patel
rump + flank — Carol Harvey Steski
How to Hold a Pebble — Jaspreet Singh
Kink Bands — David Martin
Attic Rain — Samantha Jones
Dreams of the Epoch & the Rock — Jaspreet Singh
The Beauty of Vultures — Wendy McGrath & Danny Miles
ALL WRONG HORSES ON FIRE THAT GO AWAY IN THE RAIN — Sarain Frank Soonias
Contraband Bodies — Jide Salawu
Duckweed 浮萍 — Kathryn Lennon
The Time of the Earth — Jaspreet Singh

¶ This book has been typeset in Minion Pro, designed by Robert Slimbach.

Written, edited, designed, published, and printed by humans in Canada.

JASPREET SINGH's most recent poetry books form the "Still Astonished" trilogy — *How to Hold a Pebble* (2022), *Dreams of the Epoch & the Rock* (2024) and *The Time of the Earth* (2026). More and more his work engages with deep time and the ecological.